The Evil Within: The Spiritual Battle in Your Mind

Dan Desmarques

Published by 22 Lions Bookstore, 2019.

Copyright Page

The Evil Within: The Spiritual Battle in Your Mind

By Dan Desmarques

Copyright © Dan Desmarques, 2019 (1st Ed.). All Rights Reserved.

Published by 22 Lions Bookstore and Publishing House

About the Publisher

About the 22 Lions Bookstore:

www.22Lions.com

Facebook.com/22Lions

Twitter.com/22lionsbookshop

Instagram.com/22lionsbookshop

Pinterest.com/22lionsbookshop

Introduction

Our world is changing very fast, and many believe, not in the right direction. But the weapons of evil are subtle and hard to detect, even by the most advanced religious groups. This planet is organized in such a way that most people won't be able to notice how they are being played towards their own destruction, for most of their beliefs are not even their own. But, in this book, you will understand which strategies are being used by the dark spiritual forces operating on the planet to destroy humanity, and realize how you can escape from this unseen war, being played in our minds every single day.

The Five Layers of Reality

People tend to think that they are seeing reality but actually they are seeing a combination of beliefs — collective consciousness manifested at a vibrational and physical level. They think they understand reality but actually what they understand are their own prejudices and assumptions, previously filtered by the social beliefs. They think they understand others but they are actually getting the result of their behaviors — also known as karmic laws in application. And many times people are merely confirming what they already expected to have, and not more than that. To expect more than that, you would have to change your own belief-system, and in doing so, change yourself too. And that's a challenge most humans aren't willing to have.

That is how people enter the comfort zone, in which they have friends in whom to trust, friends telling them what they want to believe, and what they always expect to hear. And such other people are living in a comfort zone too, made out of illusions. The overall suffering comes exactly from that spectrum of reality, and not from reality itself as a whole, which is neutral. In fact, part of this reality is also found in nature, the birds, the trees, the butterflies, and we can't become aware of all that when immersed in our own paradigms.

There are both positive and negative outcomes in all interactions. But those who perceive more negativity than positivity, can't really perceive a realistic outcome from any interaction. They are perceiving not what is mathematically correct, but what fits their own personal illusions and expectations. Their mental computations are made with emotional abstractions rather than factual events.

Now, is being realistic something impossible to accomplish with a common human mind? I can't really say so. Because, above that level of reality, there are other levels. And these levels are known only to a few, which typically fall lost inside of them. These are the levels of goal achievement, power, and magic.

The level of goal achievement is what you hear many motivational speakers talking about. It's about setting a goal and working hard to achieve it. And that goal can be anything in life. And it's perfectly noble of you to decide which goal you wish to have, not only in finances but also emotions. You can decide to have personal goals; You can decide to have relationship goals; You can decide to have marriage goals; Or goals in having and raising children. You can play with life at many levels and with many variables. But you do need to have a goal, to know in which direction to move. It's like buying a plane ticket; unless you know where you are going, you will never buy it; unless you decide where you want to go, you won't buy it. And interestingly enough, many people struggle with making decisions, because they are incapable of setting goals in their life. They are so afraid of doing mistakes that they become incapable of setting goals. And so, they need to know this — how to set a goal and how to plan for it. And to know it, you need something else, which is a belief in yourself — confidence rooted in self-esteem. Without these two things, you can't set goals.

If you don't believe in yourself and don't love yourself enough, you can't set goals for the future and move towards the achievement of such goals. That's what lack of motivation really is — lack of discipline and lack of self-esteem. You cannot increase your financial account and your social account without an equally rich emotional account.

Above this level, you have two more, both of them connected to hope, faith and magic. In these two upper levels, you don't just decide based on what you believe or see, or even what you want. You decide based on what you feel and your imagination, and with spiritual ambitions too. That is why few people know these upper levels; They're the god levels. But those who reach them become confused because of their ego; they think it means becoming as a god. But it's not exactly the same thing. You're cooperating with God, and not being Him or competing with Him. You're also not being less human but actually exploring your full potential as a human being, which is limitless.

Your own DNA, as scientific research has already shown, changes with your own thoughts. And if your DNA can change, if your own thinking patterns can change, there's no limit to who you can become when using the decisive power coming from your awareness.

The Highest Spiritual Level

In the upper spiritual levels, you are looking at reality as an illusion. And you understand that reality is nothing more than an illusion. But there are two types of illusion: the realistic illusion and the delusional illusion. The delusional illusion comes from you, your subconscious mind. It's about those moments when you try to escape events and experiences, but they then repeat themselves again. Because whatever you fear, you do attract. The realistic illusion is about when you trap yourself in the desires of others; when you think that a bigger house, more money and a bigger car, will set you free from all your problems; and yet, you're just playing someone else's game by doing that, rather than living your own life and getting to know your spiritual identity.

Above these levels you have others, and these magic levels are very subtle, because they're related to your spirit, they're related to who you are; and there are things you can't see or experience, because they're related to creating possibilities that seem impossible, and experiences that seem unachievable. And you move to these higher levels by experiencing them inside your mind, by creating a reality inside your mind — using your imagination. That is what magic is.

Once you do that, you will understand happiness and also the purpose of being spiritual. Because you will literally start noticing how reality is shaped by your thoughts and the subconscious level of your awareness about yourself. The world will literally show you both things.

In this upward climbing, you're not becoming a god, but instead cooperating with God, because as you experience these higher levels, you will also see the path that God has created for you more clearly and what He wishes you to learn.

To give you an example, I have used this power first to attract money and then to attract love. I attracted money with challenges that made me want to write about them, and that's how I became an author. I thought that my life was going nowhere because I kept losing all the money I got, despite all the work I invested in by having multiple jobs, until I became rich as an author and without having to need any job anymore for the rest of my life.

As what regards love, I noticed that all my girlfriends had the same behavior pattern, which resembled me a lot of my own mother, with whom I never had a good connection with. The lack of connection with someone who is mentally ill, however, was not the issue here. I had to forgive myself and forgive her, by understanding what made my own mother so evil towards me. And certainly, being with women showing the same traits, forced me to first find the answers and then study the topic extensively to avoid repeating it.

After fifteen years reading dozens of books on exorcism, psychiatry, psychology, and everything else in between, namely, gnostic writings drawing a parallel between the physical world and the world of the spirits, I eventually had no more doubts that I was dealing with cases of demonic possession. Sleeping with these women every day, and having the signs in front of me, exactly as described by exorcists, certainly erased any doubts I could still have. Even more when I noticed how much they knew about things they couldn't possibly know. For all the fights these women created happened exactly when I was in the middle of important books, that they did not even know I was writing. Books about love, moral and ethics have always instigated the worst quarrels to make me stop from finishing them, even with physical violence. And when that wasn't possible, with seduction.

As I type this book, one of my former girlfriends has been constantly texting me messages offering me sex, to hook me back and stop me from finishing it. I am not saying that she consciously knows what she is doing, but that the demon controlling her certainly does; and through different mechanics, demons know how to pressure someone into certain behaviors.

The Spiritual Deception

Demons can control a person's mind with images, which she will assume to be her own. These images, then stimulate emotions and memories, creating a chain reaction, that can even lead to insomnia. And indeed, when I am withdrawing or writing an important book, these women suffer with sleepless nights and an avalanche of thoughts bursting in their head 24 hours a day. They are being tortured and manipulated to contact me and to be with me. Because, well, they are Satan's whores.

This process isn't very different from what influential people do when wanting to buy political favors with prostitution. In fact, such women tend to be sold as Satan's whores in a gradual spiritual manner of self-imposed decadent behaviors, such as promiscuity.

In this sense, the common idea that Narcissists view their victims as property is not completely realistic. What really happens is that they view themselves as property of the evil within them, and their victim as the purpose of their existence. The Narcissists are merely the channel for something much stronger than their own predatory will. That is why the understanding of this scenario can be so confusing.

This brings me to another topic which has been widespread by society as fair and democratic and expanding furthermore demonic Influence. In a popular interview with a celebrity about her sexual affairs, she asked the interviewer: "If a woman that sleeps with many men is a slut, what is a man that sleeps with many women?" And to which the presenter properly replied: "A slut-maker".

Now, let's put our personal differences, in gender, politics or social views, as well as beliefs, aside, and look at this situation from a biological angle: Men can be manipulated with sex. Women, for biological reasons, can't. Because women are biologically wired to procreate only with the best males. A woman's willpower to resist sex and seduction is greater than in a man. That is why they can make conscious decisions before having sex while men can't. Men tend to be more easily fooled with seduction, even among the smartest. Historically, many secrets of war where exchanged between sides, by using prostitutes as the ideal bait.

That is also why in the metaphorical story of the Garden of Eden, it is the woman who consciously sins, while the man sins only to please the woman. In other words, through the emotional connection with a man, and using her conscious will, the woman exercised her power over a man, to destroy both.

Just like warlords have always used prostitutes to destroy their enemies, and even the most powerful prophets like Mohamed, or feared leaders, like Atila the Hun, were murdered by a woman, also Satan turns women into whores, by using men who are themselves possessed already, in order to bring humanity to its knees. And what is even more interesting about such men, is that they have all been hurt by demonically possessed women themselves. All the greatest male seducers in the world, have stories in their past of women who cheated on them, humiliated them and made them feel like garbage — rejected and unloved.

Out of anger and resentment, these men then proceed to have sex with as many women as they can, single or not (therefore repeating what was once done to them in the process), before feeling manly enough again to settle down with one, if that ever happens. Many of them feel so heartbroken that they lose faith in marriage. Can you see now how this cycle goes?

It is also not surprising that, at one point, an increasing number of them starts connecting spirituality with dating, and seeing the parallel between people who have sex with anyone and demonic possession, as their interviews and podcasts clearly show us.

As times goes by, these women then, after spending the best years of their youth whoring themselves in the world, want to be monogamous once their appearance starts fading away, and marry to a type of man who doesn't want them, ending up marrying one down the social pyramid, whom they consider inferior in value. And these men, because they diminish a woman's self-esteem and social value (which is contrary to what a woman is biologically wired to desire), end up being emotionally bullied during their entire marriage, therefore having their own self-esteem destroyed by it. Many of them are so traumatized by the experience and their divorce, that they then never want to be married again. Many commit suicide when cheated or after being divorced.

How Gender Wars Destroy Humanity

Everything in this world is very well-connected to destroy people's consciousness and bring their vibration to the lowest level possible, even make them commit suicide if possible, and which is commonly the case for men. Suicide is the number one cause of death in men. Two-thirds of the worldwide suicides are committed by men.

In other words, even though men are the most vilified by the media, they are the ones who suffer the most and the most likely to kill themselves due to emotional suffering.

Now, if you lived a thousand years ago or more, and that happened, you would be worried, since men were the first to die in the battlefield, and without them, you would basically have no way to protect yourself. Even most labour, because it required physical strength, had to be carried out by men.

In today's world, however, with all the equality given to women, made possible with the evolution we've witnessed in technology, men became irrelevant to the prosperity of a nation, and even unwelcome due to the threat they pose on tyrannic governments; for only men are willing to die for a social cause. And this is how, in the name of gender equality, humanity ended up creating gender inequality.

It is known, through several studies in psychology, that women tend to be more agreeable by nature, and this obviously makes the deaths of men desirable by anyone who seeks more power over the structure of humanity. And as humanity becomes more agreeable to unfair treatment and governmental abuse, people also lower their consciousness furthermore. It is what happens when you deny yourself the pain of introspection over behaviors and practices which you consider unethical.

At the lowest level of any life, you don't just see humans acting like parasites, focusing their entire existence on physical pleasures with food and sex, and using others for personal gratification only, but also, literally speaking, parasites, which tend to live and procreate inside these same individuals, for sharing a similar vibratory level.

It has been found, through different researches, that bacteria and parasites can only live in people of a very low vibration, which is the same as to say that we attract our own physical diseases with our actions, more than our emotions. Because that vibration is typically lowered through the actions of the parasites that we have contaminated ourselves with.

Our emotions, let us not be confused, are quite often already a consequence of our own actions and diseases, therefore reinforcing our physical state more than causing it.

For this reason, many religious organizations have always known that it is moral behavior that causes depression and unhappiness, and not the deliberate excuses we find to deny our own responsibility; I.e., our karma is directly linked to our moral actions as every ancient religious tradition, inspired on the teaching of extraterrestrials, often confused with angels and gods, have always told us.

It is also because extraterrestrials always knew about the implications of parasitic and bacterial contamination, that they have kept themselves separated from humans, and never allowed any human to enter in contact with them before first going through a peculiar set of procedures for decontamination, as every record about human interactions with aliens show us.

On the other hand, it is interesting to notice how psychiatry has led us to believe that the fear of germes is a serious mental disease, for nobody shows more mysophobia (also known as germophobia or verminophobia) than extraterrestrials from very advanced civilizations.

How Promiscuity Destroys Humanity

The previous topic becomes even more shocking once you understand that parasites can spread easily, in many ways too, such as with kissing. For this can make us wonder about the real reasons why we physically crave touch, even from strangers, and will do anything for that; or why women who are promiscuous, become depressed when not having, at least, a stranger for one night. And have you noticed that promiscuous women tend to become more easily depressed when alone and have a higher addiction to sugar? Because that is the link between moral actions, emotions, and parasitic contamination: the more immoral one is, the more contaminated one gets, and the more suicidal thoughts one will have, enrolling on a downward spiral towards the end, quite often in the form of a premature death that doctors never associate with parasitic contamination but is quite surely caused by it.

It is known that everyone is somehow infected to a higher or lower degree with parasites, but there are certainly many behaviors that increase the risk. And it is also not a coincidence that both the Bible and the Quran recommend not eating pork, for it is the most contaminated animal.

As for what concerns behaviors, we can notice that the more promiscuous someone is, the more that person will want to become. The physical and the spiritual elements, by attracting parasites into one's body, become intrinsically connected in a lower physical form.

In other words, Satan isn't best represented through a serpent but a similar living creature — a parasite. Because parasites that live inside a person will electrically and chemically spread signals that will trigger the host to want to spread them to others. That's what temptation is, both in craving for foods that damage our body and mind, and in wanting relationships that are purely based on physical contact, without any love or other emotions of a higher nature.

This topic of temptation gains a whole new level, when we realize that the most attractive men and women, for being more seductive and offered more opportunities to have sex with others, are also the most likely to carry parasites inside of them.

Promiscuity spreads diseases at various levels to society, through parasitic infestation, which diminishes the vitality of a person. When our vitality is diminished, your immune system is compromised, and once this occurs, we can literally die from anything, being cancer the most common and widespread form of death caused by a weak immune system. You cannot treat cancer naturally without strengthening your immune system first, and that implies, one way or another, killing all the bacteria and parasites that live inside of you, most of which you either contracted directly through promiscuous behaviors or an improper diet based fundamentally on pork meat, or indirectly, through any form of contact with promiscuous persons.

Nevertheless, I would go a step further in my assumption, that most likely men get their immune system contaminated after having sex with prostitutes, as much as women get the same when prostituting themselves. Because that's what sleeping with strangers is.

Despite these facts, I am always very intrigued by how people rationalize their immoral actions, as when a girl of only twenty-two years old, when asked why she had slept with dozens of men and kissed more than a hundred, said the following: "I am not a prostitute because I never accepted money."

Somehow, people now want to think that by removing one element from the equation, that makes everything else perfectly normal. And yet, promiscuous behavior also contributes to the diminishing of the self-esteem of the individual, which then translates into depressive states and suicidal thoughts; and lowers the vibrational level of a person, contributing to demonic possession, especially in women, for the reasons mentioned above.

This is why feminism, through the claims for equality, has contributed to the widespread of parasitic contamination, sexual diseases, and this, while contributing to a masculinization of the female population and the increasing death rates in men. As a result, women tend now to be more aggressive and less empathetic than many men, and are more unhappy than ever.

We should stop attributing the consequences of all this, such as the high divorce rates, or the unwillingness of men to be married, to female liberation, as such attitude will only contribute to increase the devastating implications on the world of a mindset that has nothing to do with female liberation, but quite the opposite. The increasing number of single mothers who have to work to raise a child they barely see, has certainly not liberated women, but suffocated them even more.

We can talk about female liberation when women living under oppressive political regimes are not put in jail for dancing in public or removing their burka, and when they can have the same rights as men to an education and to choosing their own husband.

How Loving Lost Souls Feels

As I can't be attacked directly, due to my own spiritual nature and beliefs, throughout all my entire life, there have always been people possessed by demons, that sough to destroy me, to stop me from doing what I am doing now. And by getting these two elements in my reality, and systematically, i.e., the spiritual attacks and my life purpose as an author growing in meaning, I finally understood what I was born to be, while forgiving myself for my past and all the negative programming I received since an early childhood to stop me from being who I am today. For now I can see how everything which was said to me, came from the mouth of Satan himself: "You are too stupid to have a normal life"; "you will always be lonely"; "you are evil"; "you don't deserve love".

These where words of my own mother under demonic possession, but many people I encounter today, and that are possessed too, do similar things, and try to stop me from continuing my work of freeing this planet from the claws of evil.

I also thought that my demonic-possessed parents were horrible enough, but being with a spouse who is possessed by a demon literally feels like having a hand-puppet next to you: When they touch you, you feel no energy, no love, no warmth in them; when they look at you, there is no life in their eyes, not direct contact, no emotions; when they speak, they are either speaking the words of others (other narcissists, i.e., demonically possessed, like them), or being played by a demonic force using them. You can barely see the real person there, because it isn't really there anymore. The real person is somewhere else.

A person who is possessed, is as conscious of her behaviors as a drunk one is. And they typically say the same things too: "I don't know why I do and speak such things"; "I don't remember doing and saying those things."

It is no surprise either, as drinking alcohol is a ritual of spiritual invocation. The word alcohol is derived from the Arabic "al-kuhl" which means "body eating spirit". Indeed, the vibration of someone under the effect of alcohol drops along with the consciousness, making it easier to become possessed.

Our bodies are vehicles for spirit, which manifests with our consciousness. When consciousness is denied, the spirit ceases manifesting and remains in the realm of the sleeping-dead, complete unconsciousness, also presented in fairytales as the Sleeping Beauty or a Snow White after eating the poisonous apple and falling into an eternal sleep.

In those moments, the self is turned less rational, with more memory blackouts, less self-control, less focus, and also more sexual, more violent, and so on. In general, this person has a reduced state of identity, and nearly to nothingness. The feeling of "being nothing" and having no self-love is very characteristic in such persons.

The individual who is possessed has only glimpses of what he or she once was. And they will often confess it too in phrases like: "Before I was completely different and could do much more"; or "I don't know what has happened to me or who I am anymore".

These statements are very interesting, because the "me" isn't there anymore. That is what really happened. The "me" only has a chance to be free to even see that when not being enslaved, like any other prisoner. His or her intervals of self-awareness are very short.

It is then no coincidence too, that we see demonic possessed individuals abusing alcohol consumption. And they tend to abuse alcohol more to quiet the voices in their head, even though they call it "having fun" or "relaxing".

You can try to explain this to such people but they won't even hear you, because, you see, most of them are also atheists, making it all too perfect for them to even have any chance whatsoever of ever being rescued. Their life is over already, even if they walk the Earth for another fifty years, like zombies, causing destruction on others and themselves.

The end of the world, contrary to popular belief, has nothing to do with wiping out most of the population with death. But with a cleansing that is necessary, for the ones living to continue on living. Very few people are alive in this world.

About the Publisher

This book was published by the 22 Lions Bookstore.
For more books like this visit www.22Lions.com.
Join us on social media at:
Fb.com/22Lions;
Twitter.com/22lionsbookshop;
Instagram.com/22lionsbookshop;
Pinterest.com/22LionsBookshop.

www.ingramcontent.com/pod-product-compliance
Lightning Source LLC
Chambersburg PA
CBHW050451010526
44118CB00013B/1785